THE GHOULS' GUIDE TO GOOD GRAMMAR

> READ THIS BOOK!
> It won't tell you everything, but it will get you started.

By **LESLIE KIMMELMAN** and Illustrated by **MARY SULLIVAN**

PUBLISHED BY SLEEPING BEAR PRESS™

At first, grammar may make your head spin.
But before long you'll find yourself learning the
GHOULS' RULES.

PERIODS (.)
QUESTION MARKS (?)
EXCLAMATION MARKS (!)

Put punctuation at the end of every sentence. Punctuation marks are little symbols that are used in writing to separate parts of a sentence and to make meaning clear. They're what let you stop for a minute to pick your nose, pop a blister, or blow a spitball.

Ghouls are good at groaning.

When you make a statement, use a **period**.

GROOOOOOOOOOOOAAAAAAAAAN
When you ask a question, use a **question mark**.
What's shaking?

To make something more exciting, or to show that someone's shouting, you should use an **exclamation mark**.

Oh no!
The grave is empty!
Grandpa's escaped again!

Look how a simple little **period** changes the meaning of this sentence:

COMMAS (,)

Commas are tricky. They have many jobs. Just like periods, they can tell you when to pause, but they come in the middle of a sentence, not at the end.
Commas can separate items in a list.

Oh boo! Brains, guts, and blood again.

I Lunch ticket

Commas can help make the meaning of your words clear.

Time to eat, Sylvester.

Time to eat Sylvester.

Time to eat, Sylvester
means something very
different from
Time to eat Sylvester.

And look what a **comma** does here.

Vanessa Vampire loves cooking, her parents, and her baby sister.

Uh-oh! Without commas, Vanessa's family is in big trouble!

Vanessa Vampire loves cooking her parents and her baby sister.

HYPHENS (–) AND QUOTATION MARKS (" ")

Hyphens can help change a ghoul chasing werewolf into a ghoul-chasing werewolf.

(The hyphen turns *ghoul-chasing* into a word that describes the word that comes after it.

What kind of werewolf is it? The kind that chases ghouls!)

Quotation marks are used for dialogue, before and after someone speaks.
Be careful where you put them!

"The teacher," moans the zombie, "will taste delicious!"

The teacher moans, "The zombie will taste delicious!"

CONTRACTIONS (')

Contractions are two words shortened and combined with an apostrophe to make one word.
The **apostrophe** takes the place of a letter or two.

POSSESSIVES

Possessives use apostrophes, too. But they have a different job to do. They show ownership. Where you put the apostrophe can make a big difference!

Ghoul's really gross bedroom.

The room belongs to just one ghoul.

Ghouls' really gross bedroom.

Many ghouls share this bedroom.

CAPITALIZATION

There are lots of rules to tell you when to **capitalize** the **first letter of a word**. **Days** of the week and **months** of the year are **capitalized**—but seasons are not.

The best day of the year is **O**ctober 31, which comes every fall.

Welcome to **T**ransylvania!

Place names, such as **towns**, **countries**, and **continents**, are **capitalized**.

You don't capitalize someone's job, even when it's someone important.

But if you're talking directly to that person or using a name, use a capital letter.

I am the king of the vampire bats!

Welcome, **King Ludwig**, ruler of the vampire bats.

It's the witch!

That's **Witch** Brunhilda to you.

FIENDISH FOOLERS

Some word pairs are great tricksters.

A ghoul loves **its** lunch.

Its shows possession.

Unless **it's** an onion.

It's is a contraction, meaning *it is*.

Who's is a contraction, meaning *who is*.
Whose asks who it belongs to.

Then is used to show the order of things happening—*first*, *then*, and so on.

They're is a contraction, meaning *they are*.

They're doing the tombstone tango.

There means *at that place*. **Their** is possessive, meaning *it belongs to them*.

You're is a contraction, meaning *you are*.

Your is possessive, meaning *something belongs to you*.

The three billy goats
passed over the ogre.

Now the three billy goats
are a thing of the past.

Passed is an action; the goats went over.

Past refers to time.

AND WATCH OUT FOR HOMOPHONES!

They are words that *sound the same* but have different spellings and different meanings.

Beware: cold **stairs**

Hair-raising

The end of the **tail**

Beware: cold **stares**

Hare-raising

The end of the **tale**

I'm going to the monster library for a copy of my favorite book.

MONSTER LIBRARY

Me too.

Two books are better than one!

To, too, and two can be confusing.
To means *approaching* or *going toward*, too means *also*,
and two is a *number*.

You've done it!

You've reached the ~~ghoul~~ goal line!

DON'T let what you've learned o o o o o z e out of your brain.

You've mastered some important grammar rules for ghouls (not to mention other monstrous creatures).

And that means, we've come to . . .

The end?

Yes, the end!

Goodbye!

Which of these sentences has **no mistakes**?
Go back and read through the book if you need help.

1. Someone asked the ghoul, "What are you're favorite foods?"

2. The ghoul giggled. "My favorite foods are fried flies, toenail tacos, and YOU!"

3. Uh-oh! The ghouls favorite foods are fried flies, toenail tacos, and YOU!

4. A hungry zombie chimed in. "Cool! Those are my favorite foods two!"

The correct answer is number 2. But why are you still here? Unless you want to be lunch for zombies,

RUN!!!!

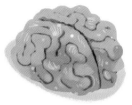

To Barb, a wonderful editor who elevates each book she works on
and who knows just where to place every punctuation mark. Thank you!
—Leslie

To my dad
—Mary

SLEEPING BEAR PRESS™

2395 South Huron Parkway,
Suite 200, Ann Arbor, MI 48104
www.sleepingbearpress.com
© Sleeping Bear Press

Printed and bound in the United States
10 9 8 7 6 5 4 3 2 1

Library of Congress Cataloging-in-Publication Data
Names: Kimmelman, Leslie, author. | Sullivan, Mary, 1958- illustrator.
Title: The ghouls' guide to good grammar / by Leslie Kimmelman and illustrated by Mary Sullivan.
Description: Ann Arbor, MI : Sleeping Bear Press, [2021] | Audience: Ages 4-8. | Summary: "Monsters such as zombies, werewolves, and
ghouls explain basic rules of grammar, including correct punctuation, appropriate word choices, and contractions"— Provided by publisher.
Identifiers: LCCN 2021005304 | ISBN 9781534110953 (hardcover)
Subjects: LCSH: English language—Grammar—Juvenile literature. | Monsters—Juvenile literature.
Classification: LCC PE1112 .K48 2021 | DDC 428.2—dc23
LC record available at https://lccn.loc.gov/2021005304